MUSICAL
INSTRUMENTS
OF THE WORLD

Flutes

M. J. Knight

W
FRANKLIN WATTS
LONDON•SYDNEY

 An Appleseed Editions book

First published in 2005 by Franklin Watts
96 Leonard Street, London, EC2A 4XD

Franklin Watts Australia
45-51 Huntley Street, Alexandria, NSW 2015

© 2005 Appleseed Editions

Created by Appleseed Editions Ltd,
Well House, Friars Hill, Guestling, East Sussex, TN35 4ET

Designed by Helen James

ISBN 0 7496 5845 2

A CIP catalogue for this book is available from the British Library.

Photographs by Corbis (Tony Arruza, Tiziana and Gianni Baldizzone, Derick A.
Thomas; Dat's Jazz, Ric Ergenbright, Werner Forman, John Henley, Wolfgang Kaehler,
Kelly-Mooney Photography, Earl & Nazima Kowall, Bob Krist, LWA-Dann Tardif,
Buddy Mays, Michael Maslan Historic Photographs, Royalty-Free, Michael St. Maur
Sheil, Ariel Skelley, Paul A. Souders, Ted Spiegel, David Turnley, Nik Wheeler),
Photri (US Navy photo by Jessica Davis), Sergio Piumatti, John Walmsley

Printed in Thailand

Contents

Introducing flutes

Flutes Flutes Flutes

This book is about flutes, which belong to the woodwind family of instruments.

These instruments create a sound when the air inside them vibrates. The player either blows into, or across, the instrument's mouthpiece to create notes. The sound each instrument makes depends on how long it is. The longer the instrument, the lower the notes it plays.

These Chinese flute players are marching in a parade in Cheung Chau, Hong Kong.

4

Most early woodwind instruments were made of wood, but today many are made of metal or plastic.

Children practise together playing a variety of different wind instruments.

You can hear some of these instruments playing classical music in an orchestra. The woodwind section of an orchestra includes flutes and a piccolo, playing alongside clarinets, oboes, bassoons, and sometimes a saxophone.

Other flutes play traditional or classical music from many different parts of the world, or can be heard in dance, folk, rock, pop and jazz bands.

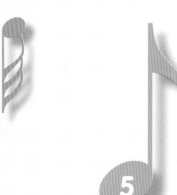

Early flutes Early flutes

Can you imagine how the first flutes were made? Thousands of years ago, when people lived in caves, someone had the idea of hollowing out the bones of a deer or a bear, which had been cooked and eaten. Next he tried blowing through the hollow bones to see whether they made a sound. Soon, people discovered they could make different notes if they pierced holes in the sides of the bones.

Did you know?

A 45,000-year-old flute was found in a cave in Eastern Europe. It had been made from the leg bone of a bear, had four finger holes, and, amazingly, could still be played!

From these early beginnings come many of the flutes we play today. In Central and South America people made flutes from the tiny bones of birds. Later, people began to create flutes from clay and wood.

This flute was carved in Peru from an animal bone. It has a bird's head at one end.

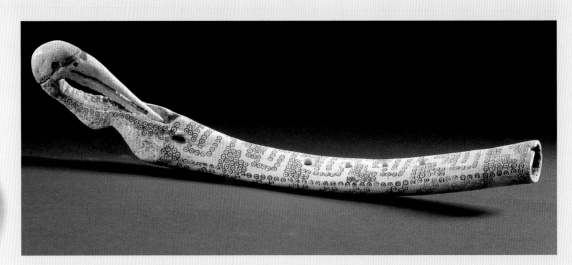

Bird whistle
Bird whistle
Bird whistle
Bird whistle
Bird whistle
Bird whistle
Bird whistle

True to its name, this flute makes a low warbling sound, rather like birdsong.

You need to fill the whistle with water before you play it. When you blow down the spout, the air bubbles through the water and out through a small hole to make a warbling note.

Some bird whistles are made from clay or metal, but you can also buy toy plastic bird whistles, which sound a higher note. Perhaps you have one?

To play this whistle, you fill it with water and blow into the bird's tail.

Tin whistle

Tin whistle Tin whistle Tin whistle

Another name for the tin whistle is the penny whistle. The name comes from the pennies people used to give musicians who played their instruments in the street. Today street musicians are known as buskers.

Tin whistles are made of thin metal. They have six finger holes and no thumb hole, so they are quite easy to play.

You can hear dance or folk bands play lively jigs and reels on tin whistles. Their bright, high-pitched sound makes people want to tap their feet and dance.

This tin whistle player is part of a folk band playing at a music festival in Ireland.

Flageolet Flageolet Flageolet

The flageolet is a whistle flute which makes a high, shrill sound. More than a hundred years ago French and English musicians played flageolets in bands and orchestras. They played the highest notes in a piece of music.

These early flageolets had a nozzle mouthpiece, which held a small piece of sponge. This soaked up the saliva from the player's mouth.

Today you can buy toy flageolets in different sizes. They are made of metal, but have a plastic mouthpiece.

This toy flageolet has a green plastic mouthpiece and six finger holes.

Recorders

Recorders

Are you learning to play the recorder? Did you know that there are five different types?

The smallest is the sopranino, a tiny recorder with finger holes very close together. Next comes the descant recorder, which is the one most often played in schools.

These girls are playing descant recorders at an outdoor concert in Prague, Czech Republic.

You can see the curved metal crook on the bass recorder in the middle of this group. On either side are the tenor and treble recorder.

Treble and tenor recorders are bigger and lower-sounding, but the deepest of all is the bass recorder. This is so big that it has an extra part: a curved metal tube called a crook, which helps players to reach the finger holes while blowing.

Recorders have been played in Europe for about a thousand years. The first recorders were made from a single piece of wood or ivory, but today they are built in three sections, which can be wooden or plastic.

The soft, clear sound of a recorder is perfect for playing solo pieces or playing in small groups.

11

Recorders

Nose flute
Nose flute Nose flute

Imagine an instrument you play through your nose!
This is how the nose flute is played.

This way of playing started in Polynesia in the Pacific
Ocean, because the people who lived there believed that
the breath from your nose had special magic powers.

Nose flute players close one nostril with a finger or a piece
of cloth when they play. Their flutes are made of bamboo
and have three finger holes which the player covers to
make different notes.

*This Polynesian man
holds one nostril
closed and blows
into his flute through
the other one.*

12

Bosun's pipe Bosun's pipe

Sailors play this tiny metal pipe when they welcome people on board ship.

The player holds the pipe in one hand and blows into the mouthpiece. Her breath hits a small hole at the end of the pipe and makes a loud whistling sound.

To change the note the pipe makes, the sailor opens and closes her hand. She wears the pipe on a cord around her neck.

This sailor is using her fingers to change the note as she plays her bosun's pipe.

Bosun's pipe   Bosun's pipe

13

Ring flute Ring flute

True to its name, this flute has a ring of dried palm leaves wrapped around one end. When the player blows into the flute, the ring of leaves helps to channel the breath into the blow hole.

This bamboo flute comes from Indonesia. It has six finger holes and can be a variety of different lengths. The ring flute is also called the suling. It is usually played as part of a group of mainly percussion instruments called a gamelan orchestra.

The ring flute is played to accompany special dances in Bali, Indonesia.

Double flute Double flute

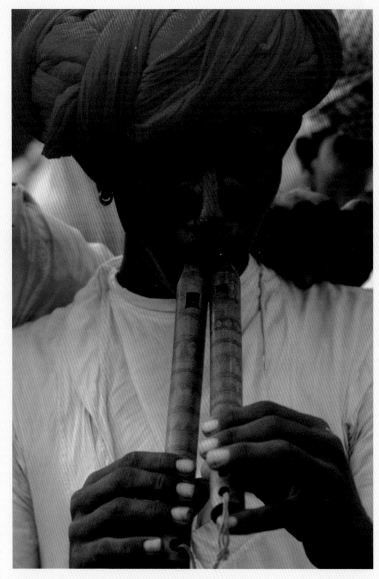

Double flutes are two flutes in one. Some are carved from one piece of wood, while others are made by tying two pipes tightly together.

Players can perform two tunes at the same time – one on each pipe. If the pipes are different lengths they play in different pitches – one higher than the other.

Many double flutes come from Eastern Europe. Ancient clay flutes have been found in South America and Mexico which have three or four pipes. The pipes are joined up so the air goes into all of them at the same time.

This double flute player from Rajasthan in India is wearing a red turban on his head.

Panpipes are a series of tiny flutes of different lengths, joined together in a raft shape. Each pipe plays only one note; the short pipes play higher notes than the long pipes.

A panpipe player blows across the top of each pipe in turn by moving her head or the pipes. The lower end of the pipes is sealed.

Did you know?

Panpipes were named after a Greek god called Pan. People believed that Pan invented the pipes to play to a goddess he loved called Syrinx.

A Peruvian piper plays her panpipes at Venice Beach in California.

Panpipes can be made of clay, stone, wood, metal or plastic. They are played all over the world. The first panpipes were played in Ancient Greece more than 3,000 years ago, and they spread from there throughout Europe.

A band of pipers and drummers from the Aymara tribe in Bolivia, South America.

Today the light, reedy sound of the panpipes is most often heard in South American folk bands. The pipes can be many different sizes. The largest are more than 2 metres long, and slant away from the player to rest on the ground.

Concert flute

Concert flute

Do you know how many parts a concert flute has? The answer is three: the head joint, the middle joint and the foot joint. They allow the flautist (the name for a flute player) to take the instrument apart to carry it around.

The mouthpiece has a lip plate over a blow hole. The flautist rests her lips on this to play. She blows across, and not into, the blow hole to make a note.

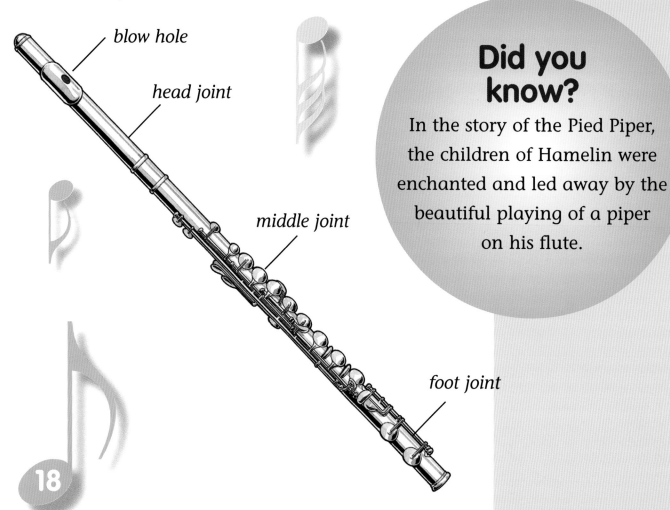

blow hole

head joint

middle joint

foot joint

Did you know?

In the story of the Pied Piper, the children of Hamelin were enchanted and led away by the beautiful playing of a piper on his flute.

The concert flute has several keys, which look like small metal caps, on the middle joint. The flautist holds these down to make different notes.

These two girls are playing the flute in their school band.

The concert flute plays in the wind section of an orchestra. Its highest notes are strong and bright, while its low notes are round and mellow.

The first flutes were wooden, but today most flutes are made of metal: there are even silver and gold flutes.

Alto flute and bass flute

The alto flute plays rounded, sad-sounding notes. It looks like the concert flute, but is larger, and plays deeper notes.

Lower still is the bass flute. This large instrument is very heavy, and so long that it is bent round at one end so that the flautist can reach all the finger holes.

These two flutes sometimes play in the wind section of an orchestra, but are not usually played as solo instruments.

Did you know?

If you straightened out a bass flute, it would be 130 centimetres long.

Eddie Parker plays his bass flute at a jazz festival in England.

The baby of the flute family, the piccolo, is just half as big as the concert flute.

The piccolo plays the highest notes in an orchestra. Sometimes it plays a higher version of the tune the violins or flutes are playing. Despite its small size, it has a loud sound, which can be heard above all the other instruments.

Piccolo players hold their instrument in the same way as the concert flute, and blow air gently across the blow hole to sound a note.

This piccolo player belongs to a marching band in Maryland, USA.

Did you know?

Piccolo is an Italian word that means small.

21

Flutes in concert

The sound of an orchestra is created by many different instruments. They are divided into four sections: strings, woodwind, brass and percussion.

Flutes play an important part in the woodwind section, which usually has several flutes and a piccolo. The flautists sit behind the violas, which are part of the string section. The concert flute often plays the tune in a piece of classical music.

You can also hear the concert flute playing classical music in a wind quintet. This group of five instruments also includes an oboe, a clarinet, a bassoon and a horn.

These flautists are part of a school wind band.

Flutes can be heard in different types of traditional music too.

Ti-tzu Ti-tzu Ti-tzu

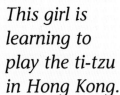

This girl is learning to play the ti-tzu in Hong Kong.

Chinese people have been playing the ti-tzu for thousands of years. It is made of bamboo and played in the same way as a western concert flute: by blowing air across the top of the blow hole.

Did you know?

The dragon flute is a ti-tzu played in religious ceremonies. It has a carved dragon's head at one end and a tail at the other, and is decorated with a shiny substance called lacquer.

The ti-tzu has nine finger holes, which the player covers to make different notes. A small piece of tissue paper is stuck over one of the finger holes, which makes a buzzing sound when the ti-tzu is played.

23

Ocarina Ocarina Ocarina

The ocarina is an unusual flute because it has a rounded shape, rather than a long, tubular one like most other flutes.

The first ocarinas were probably made in Egypt about 5,000 years ago from bones, large hollow seeds or baked earth. Today many ocarinas are made from clay or plastic.

Did you know?

The name ocarina is Italian, and means little goose. This is because in Italy ocarinas were made in the shape of a bird.

This ocarina was made by the Aztec people who lived in Mexico hundreds of years ago. It is shaped like a turtle.

Modern ocarinas are shaped like a long egg. They have a blow hole and up to eight finger holes. Small ocarinas play high notes and large ones low notes. The sound is clear and pure.

Some ocarinas have a tuning plunger, which sticks out of one end. The plunger can be pulled out or pushed in to play higher or lower notes.

To play the ocarina you blow into the blow hole and cover the other holes with your fingers

Ocarina Ocarina Ocarina

Fife Fife Fife Fife Fife Fife

Y̶ou might see fifes being played in an American or Irish marching band today. These small, narrow, wooden flutes are played in the same way as metal flutes.

Fifes usually have a blow hole and a lip plate, but are made all in one piece, unlike metal flutes.

The sound made by a fife is high and shrill, which suits the sort of music that soldiers marched to hundreds of years ago. They are often accompanied by drums.

A fife player in a marching band in Colonial Williamsburg, USA. He wears the clothes young soldiers wore 200 years ago.

26

Swannee whistle
Swannee whistle

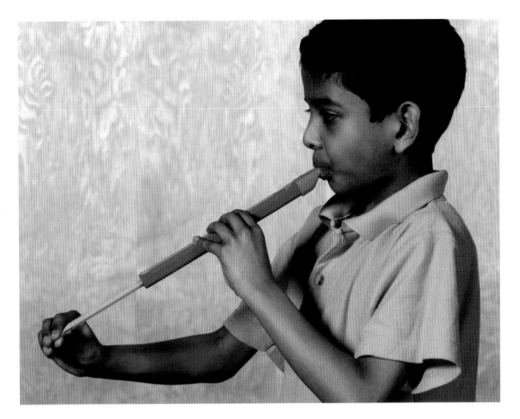

To make the swannee whistle's swooping sound you pull the plunger in and out.

Have you heard a swannee whistle? It makes an amazing swooping sound. The sound is made by part of the whistle called the plunger.

When the player pushes the plunger into the whistle and blows, the notes slide upwards. When the plunger is pulled out of the whistle, the notes slide downwards.

The whistle has no finger holes and is often played to create a sound effect. You may hear it in the music for funny films.

Shakuhachi Shakuhachi

28

Imagine what it would be like to play an instrument while wearing a basket over your head! This is what shakuhachi players had to do. The baskets were worn so that no one would recognize the players and today shakuhachi players still wear them.

This Japanese instrument is made from a piece of bamboo, which is cut near the bottom of the plant, where the stem is widest. This gives the shakuhachi a slightly curved shape.

To play the shakuhachi, the player rests it on his lower lip and blows against a notch cut into the side of the tube. He makes different notes by covering the finger holes.

Today, shakuhachi players perform both classical and folk music on their instruments.

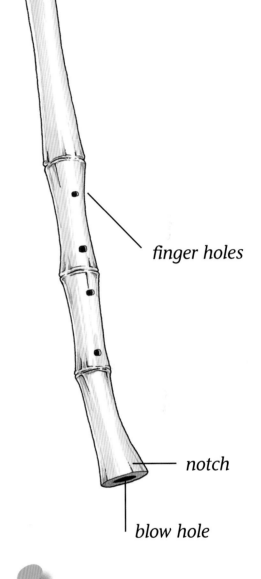

finger holes

notch

blow hole

These Japanese monks are playing their shakuhachis in the traditional way.

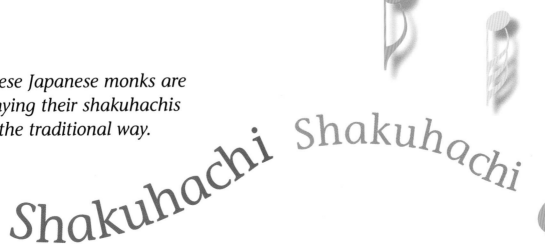

Shakuhachi Shakuhachi

Words to remember

accompany To play alongside.

bamboo A tall grass with a hollow stem which is used to make many traditional flutes and pipes.

blow hole The name of the hole a flute player blows across to make a note.

classical music Serious music is sometimes called classical music to separate it from popular music. Classical music can also mean music whicht was written during the late 18th and early 19th centuries and followed certain rules.

crook A long, thin tube on some wind instruments which helps players reach all the finger holes.

ensemble A small groups of musicians who play together.

finger holes The holes in an instrument which the player covers to make different notes.

flautists Someone who play the flute.

folk Traditional songs and tunes which are so oid that no one remembers who wrote them.

gamelan orchestra A group of instruments from Indonesia played in religious ceremonies. It can include percussion instruments, drums, fiddles, and flutes.

jazz A type of music played by a group of instruments in which each one plays its own tune. Jazz musicians often improvise, or make up, the tunes they play.

joint A section of a flute.

keys Small metal caps on a flute which cover the finger holes.

lip plate A rest for the player's lips which helps him or her blow across the blow hole when playing.

marching band A groups of musicians who march as they play. Most marching bands play music that was originally played by soldiers.

mellow Gentle and warm.

mouthpiece The part of a wind instrument which the player puts in his or her mouth and blows into.

musicians People who play instruments or sing.

notch A cut at the top of some flutes which is shaped like a U or a V. A notch makes the flute easier to play.

orchestra A group of about 90 musicians playing classical music together.

pitch How low or high a sound is.

plunger Part of a swannee whistle (and some ocarinas) that can be pulled out or pushed in to sound different notes.

pop music Popular music that is entertaining and easy to listen to.

reedy Thin and buzzing.

rock music Pop music with a strong beat, or rhythm.

shrill High and loud.

solo A piece of music played or sung by one performer.

vibrate To move up and down very quickly, or quivers. The air inside a wind instrument vibrates when someone blows into it.